A FISTFUL *of Ponies*

Poems by
DAN PROVOST

Raw Earth Ink

2021

This book is a work of original poetry.

First paperback edition July 2021

Cover design by tara caribou

ISBN 978-1-7360417-8-9 (paperback)

Published by Raw Earth Ink
PO Box 39332
Ninilchik, AK 99639
www.taracaribou.com

Dedicated to my beautiful wife, Laura and our dog, Bella.

My thanks to the editors of the magazines where some of these poems appeared: *Deuce Troupe, Medusa's Kitchen, Live Nude Poems, Dumpster Fire Press, Rye Whiskey Review,* and *Ariel Chart.*

You're 59 years old. The search is still on.
Search for what?
You want to keep that an open-ended question.

A fistful of ponies suddenly has become one
dying dog on a chain. Alternatives were always
provided, now

you are fed scraps when thought of—then left to
fend for yourself.

but you are captured, running free is scarcely an
option anymore.
The time to find that *something* is running out.

Quite Simply

--And when the shadows began
to creep into the city…

Situations arise, where names
are not important…

Castles of catastrophes added.

Fate, time and
fatigue…

--are all that's left.

Pained Writing

Force the issue and
you will surely die.

Plus, I have no firsthand experience
with porcelain plates or diamond studded
lovers who left me at
the alter.

I know this.
I understand this.
But still
dream
anyways.

Did We Ever Dance?

I always feared the devil
but did succumb to his
dances with the orchestra

many times.

Maybe you
were with me?

I Was in Love Once

Once — 3:30 PM alone with the tracer of daffodils and sunflowers mearing your far shoulder. She is innocent, she is beautiful… Her simplicity cannot be touched by human hands… A sighting of love streams along the valley with the call of sweetness ringing in your soul… Trying to be heard on this day somewhere, somehow… to scream I love.

I feel….

Seasonal Affective Disorder

I wish a
walk in the park
could turn into
 a biopic.

Too bad my head
continues to stare
down—

Snow in March…

Dreary
wind
—no need to film…
Just despicable here.

Sit a Spell

John Dorsey
enlightened me to
the fact that dilapidated
houses in northern New
England can be worshipped,

while listening to *Gimme Shelter*,

was not just a
convenient irony.

Statement from a Syllabus

Classic Literature is
insanity feeling good at the
moment of its conception.

No Notice Today

Only a poor, sad life
gone, with no fanfare...
No kindly observation
of depressed tryst
with villains, heroes and
fools...

That was That

--As quick as beauty entered,

she left.

Her obedience was
conquered with his

quick nod and
sold
tongue.

I'm Guilty

Too many little
philosophical observers out
there—calling themselves
writers, repeating everything
that has been said.

Don't hide your head, I do
the same god damn thing.

Why I Will Never Go to Another High School Reunion

Was disappointed when I discovered
many of my old high-school chums
are blatant racist from misspelled
facebook posts.

Not surprised, however.

Do Not Make "it" Cool

Funny, I see the term
"glorious agony" —

While reading bio's
about dead writers.

Wipe the sweat from
my forehead,
then cry like a baby.

No heroics for my demise...

What Caring Really Means

Empathy…not situational sorrow.

Faith in Something Bigger

Finality
starts
by
staring at the ocean.
Encompassing your world
one wave at a time.
Filling the soul with
a
thought
of something bigger
than
 you…

I'll Pass

I see that famous 70's band
is reuniting and playing some gigs.

The old, broken bones tour.
Begging to be relevant again…
Losing—

Chucky-ish

It wasn't a soft place to
go. Just an establishment to
gain courage.

Naturally shy, morose—ready
for a tasty lyric from the juke
to erase my lingering
                    doldrums.

I am a haven here.
My spells of absurdity are cured here.
The other patrons leave me alone here.

Am I sounding too Chucky-ish?

Suggestions are usually ignored.

Tough Figuring Out

Sartre told me that death cannot be
assimilated into human consciousness.

Camus than interrupted — saying, *"suicide is
the true philosophical question."*

Trump then screamed to his minions…
"I alone can fix it…"

All I can do is cover my face and say —

Gosh.

What's That, Friedrich?

Charred spiritually, not
because I spoke to Zarathustra
about God being alive or dead —

I just wondered
who killed him
or her, or---

whatever?

Orange Driver Revisited

Eddie Burns sang that
I would be acting like her clown
while she spent all my money.

Then the J.Geils Band repeated
the same warning ten years later.

I had trouble believing Peter Wolf.
Even though Magic Dick gave a
great
blues harp solo…

Gone so Fast

Aloof from my vision.
Dead from a transition…

Since the commuter rail left town within
an airborne inquiry of why.

Just another misspoke/mishap
that shakes me to a vexed core.

Keep me Posted so I'll Feel Good When I Punch You in the Mouth

Those who feel themselves despised
do well to look despising.
--Huxley, Brave New World

Tell me an awful tale
before content becomes
                    appealing.

Hatred inspired,
so I can
internally justify my daily
dose of madness.

Beautiful Insomnia

Dog-tired satisfied
but still not sleeping.

Know I'll be up all night,
sit in my comfortable chair,
and just listen

and just be.

My place in eternity

correctly captured.

OK

It is, I guess
a fair place to find
an alliance with dying.
The cold, dark bedroom,
sheets and linen not washed
in weeks.
Smell of must--soiled body
entrapped through walls.
Then nothing...
A slice of dawn passes through the window.
The ultimate equalizer
of end...

Found for Today

There are thoughts that
are beautiful,
silent…
Displayed with only
a passing glance that
declares so much love
in an instant.
Then
a hand to hold.
Peace.
Tender–an uncontrollable
urge to weep.
The tears of laughter; man & woman.
We have searched
and found.

DAN PROVOST

Asking for a Friend

Just adding to the bottom
of a bucket.

What lies beneath, a discarded
collection?

Mama

Remembered a crying
mother, kneeling in the
ocean...

Screams of anguish and fear,
trying to console a
world of hurt:

"We were the *ones*
       who wept over children—"

She muttered.

Demons kept marching.

Not listening.

Gazebo

One tender moment with her.
A bow—a dance,
quiet reflection
and atonement
for despair
never understood.

Not Science Fiction

Head still
staggered...

Tilted—
Far away from all the
terror you
        have seen...

Self-inflicted
...

Maybe, maybe not.

A Final Thought

Last words
read were by
Kell Robertson.

"Failed
   Moved on
Always another
last chance."

Put the book down,
shuttered—then I
left this world…

A far better
   man than an
hour ago.

Better Than the Dictionary

Had no clue what requiem meant
until I watched Jared Leto and
Ellen Burstyn teetering on the
fringe of sanity &
death...

Selby told me, in detail, later on--

How lament and failure is
just another outlet of

human nature.

Even the gods refuse
to intervene when that
superstar, Mr. Bones,

comes knocking on
your back door.

DAN PROVOST

On the Left

Swank
seductive bar-whores
basking in drunken glory.
Observing depravity in flight.
Hazed by sullen dankness that
flows within the next shot glass.
A faithful scene scattered about in the crusty city.

Where accepted mourners stare.

Forget-Him-Not

The crippled guy
who crawls in the rain.

No shirt or shoes.

Just a brick to help
him stammer down the road.

A crowd of disinformed watch
the struggles.

Umbrellas up…

The crippled guy
who crawls in the rain.

Asks for nothing—
Given less—

A staple of nothingness
in raggedy skin.

Witnessed as a lamppost
or a street sign.

Ready to fade.
Nothing to be said.

No philosophical question will
be asked about his plight.

He is war-torn,
invalid—

Too worthless
to bury.

To frightened
to care...

Pete Again

"I had enough of living."
The Who

Just to escape for
one day from the
embrace of dying arms.

Too much to ask?

Welcomed Sadness

Melancholy achieved while
listening to Sgt. Pepper's Lonely
Hearts Club Band.

She is leaving home, Paul.

And, like the good book says--

We all get to leave
soon enough...

Excitement for an Offensive Lineman

Pulling down the line of
scrimmage—then knocking
the shit out of a guy who was
purposely unblocked is
called a trap play…

Try it sometime…
It's orgasmic…

DAN PROVOST

Near Christmas

Also...
With a view of some
cheap Nirvana in my soul.

I will seek and find nothing...

ZZ Top sang Jesus Just Left Chicago once

Maybe he'll end up
on Watson Avenue—looking for
revenge for all the mortal
sins
  I
    have
      committed...

The blinking Christmas lights
are worn on the triple-decker apartments.

Lower world seeking Jesus joy...

I will walk among restless purgatory engorged
imposters
and wait for the Son of God to confront me...

I hope he is in a good mood.

Pollock's Art

Genius in ruffled lines…stripped of facsimile.
Somewhat fractured.

So engulfed in pastoral non-unity, a visceral of
the dots by satellite.

Endless colored roads or power…streams living,

dying,

redirecting.

Bulging into the depths.

Painful.

Unwanted Blubber

This is a personal statement.
Sanctioned by no-one really--
Climbing over the hill, sun
indirectly causes a bloody
scorn that he/she applies
to my crackpot face.

Panting away over the
useless excursion, frothing
at the hips for one more self-appointed
go round.
Lies always replace middle-age glory.

Why?

The cat was dead.
The dog was shot.

I took a long time
walking nowhere that day.

Hands in my pockets,
hoodie over my bald plate.

Light snow—tried
to cut the prelude.

The pets were gone...again,
I was alone.

To bury or burn my
poor...my steps
did nothing be leave me
ashamed.

I teared again.

DAN PROVOST

Chewed on a fingernail,
took down my hoodie

And told anyone who
was listening —

I was never god.

Not Tempting

Does your temptation
rage when you
close your eyes?

I never saw the pretty
girl fasting for size 1
incorporated.

He was on the other
side of the room, just envisioning tenderness
in a storm of unity.

Yea, right…

She was a catch-22 while
being beaten by the boys.

Yea, wrong…

To struggle with
depth is no reward…

Yea, sure…

Give the lady something to eat…
A bucket to vomit in.

Give that guy some Zoloft,
maybe a dirty prayer.

Just seems so outlandish
sometimes.

The seat, the stare—

The dark brake into
the
storm.

Admittance of it

This is an admittance of
guilt.

Of wanting to say something—

But not being able to phrase *it* correctly.

99% of the shit I write, has the word *it*
in italics.

Why?

We do not know what it is.

Is it a villain?
Is it existence?
Is it the last door we open?

All of us have a claim of it…we
just cannot find
an adequate definition
of
it…

It
Shit
However anyone wants to
perceive it…

Could be a phantom.
Or just sadness.

My it is not the
same as your it

Look at me…
Me at look.

It's how you use "it"

Isn't it?

Looking Through the Gate

Self-hatred agendas
are high on the list today

as I follow anger to the fountain…

where Lennon's flowers are singing
about looking glass ties…

Ghost of mule—tide Jim
drinking himself to death.

With no remorse or applause.

I am listening to sacred cows

who keep reminding me how
much my words

fail.

Immediate response is not
necessary.

I've given most of my life
to internal tears…
Waiting for death is just an annoyance
of trials
without tribulation.

Saw Nothing

Distracted by useless except…
white noise that buzzes when nothing
else can be heard…an emptiness of road.

Few survivors today.

Grafton Notch

The flow of noticed
travels and
sways.

Water, bouncing off
boulders toward delivery,
into a once
deleted
soul.

You Begin to Doubt

The dusty veil.
Soiled shoes.

All I have to wear is
seeds of
     misgivings.

I remember nothing.
I refuse
validity.

Fashion statements
yawn with mood rings
and man buns.

A Bargain

Five bucks for a copy
of Whitman's *Leaves of Grass*
at the local bookstore.

The strawman kid, with the art deco
bracelet behind the
counter rings the book up and
asks, "Is this new?"

I retreat into a catatonic shelter,
not ready to face the new crowd.

3 A.M. Bar Closing Conversation or
No Answers

Him-I lost my son-he was everything to me.
Me-I never had a damn thing...only what's in
front of my hands...A sight *I* often doubt.

Him-You have no idea of family, love,
tenderness?!?!
Me-Is that a question or a statement?

Him-Is this a non-linear chat?
Me-What the fuck?

Him-My son, he is gone...gone somewhere...
Me-We all go somewhere, don't we?

Him-I'm talking about after someone
dies...Heaven, Hell, Purgatory,
Me-So am I...Even if it's dangerously dark...

Him- The spirit will hopefully appear when I see
him again...
Me-What do you expect to see?

Him-An answer to why he had to leave me so
soon.
Me-We all leave my friend, some sooner than
others.

Him-Are you listening to me? My child is dead.
Me-We're all dead—the final truth we all face.

Him-Fuck you. You know what, forget it—forget
I even attempted to ta…
Me-(interrupting) I left before this conversation
even started…

Telling the Truth

Aerosmith took
me from wine to
whiskey within hearing
the first chords of
Chip Away at the Stone...

Figure I could be cool
and intellectual here...claiming
that Sinclair Lewis was the source
of my Jack Daniels improvement...

But rock and roll stays as a Lord's Prayer...

Plus lying is a mortal sin.

The Town Proverb

Obvious bad choices led
to menial radiance—becoming
the guy with seven teeth, a long rap
sheet, and a future of being found
frozen near the Town Hall.

The suburbs always has its own
failure stories—

Told by the moral mighty in
Sunday School Class.

Flying Off the Deep Depression

Frankly,
I have chosen to discard
all my former heroes
—and start from scratch.

They/them seized
my respect
by scratching at
morals I tried to
live by.

Like *they/them* had any ethics...

The truth
was, *they/them,* were
just testing my limits

of survival.

Honestly,
what one man claims to
be home—another lies
his head on solid earth

without any
forwarding address.

There is no gleaming
warrior reward for
self-involved champions.

Idols fade eventually…without
a pass or fail grade.

My new, first breath will feature
an exhale.

Opportunity to withdraw from
a craving
of immortality.

To begin anew…
Here—
Not there—

Self-worth
    slowly
    gained.

Dine with the Dark

The senses
The inner   *## outlook*

Going, gone   *## my interpretation*

Clown culture—
Withdrawn   *## my talent*
whine   *(or lack thereof)*

filmed on location
within my head…

my soul of
        nothingness…

shot the scene yesterday
where the stealers took
my pencils and
I cried my fifth grade
eyes out…   *## we are the children of*
                     therapy
                     and medication…

battered with   *## fear*
the belt…

adult—weighed   *## fear as the days left*
down   *grow shorter…*
within myself

Lorazepam, Zoloft,   *## see above, childhood*
Wellbutrin, Seroquel   *morphs into*
     dark
     adulthood

See you on   *## the beautiful language*
The other side.   *is lacking.*

About the Author

A veteran of the small press, Dan Provost's poetry has been published both in print and online for many years. He is the author of twelve books, His latest—*Darting In and Out*, will be released in May 2021 by Kung Fu Treachery Press. Dan has twice been nominated for the Best of the Net and has read his work throughout the United States. He lives in Berlin, New Hampshire with his wife Laura, and Bichon Frise, Bella.

www.ingramcontent.com/pod-product-compliance
Lightning Source LLC
Chambersburg PA
CBHW032029040426
42448CB00006B/781